PIANO *love* SONGS
FOR ADULTS

10 Most Romantic Melody
Easy Sheet Music for Beginners

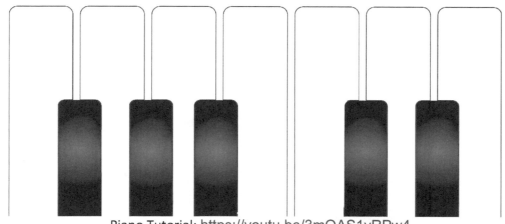

Piano Tutorial: https://youtu.be/3mOAS1vRPw4

CONTENTS

The Man I Love

George Gershwin

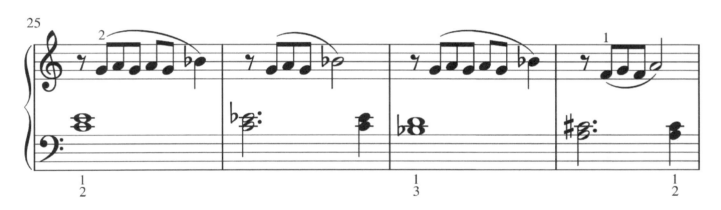

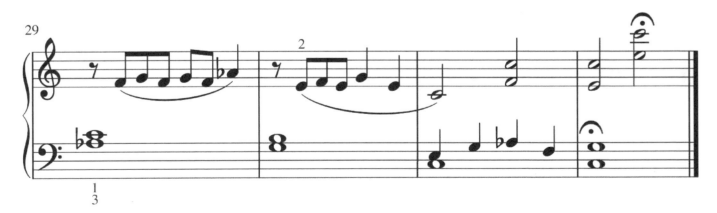

Embracaeble You

George Gershwin

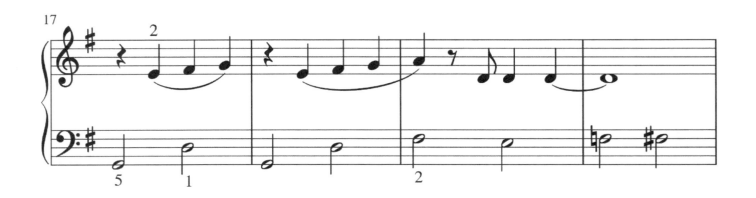

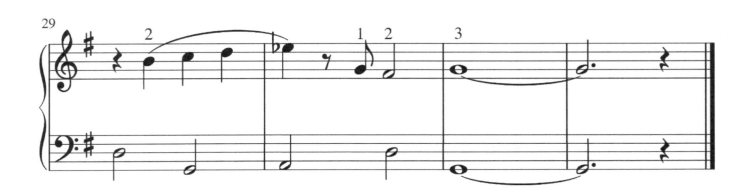

Canon in D

Johann Pachelbel

Clair de Lune

Claude Debussy

Fur Elise

Ludwig van Beethoven

Ped. simile

Moonlight Sonata

Ludwig van Beethoven

Serenade

Franz Schubert

21

O Mio Babbino Caro

from Gianni Schicchi

Giacomo Puccini

2

Liebestraum

from Nocturne No. 3

Franz Liszt

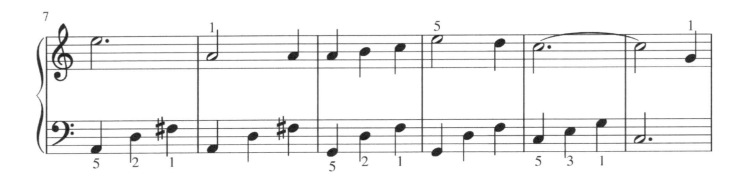

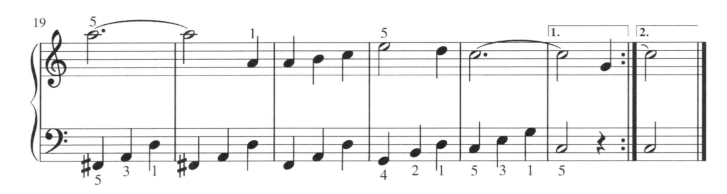

Salut d'Amour

Edward Elgar

Ped. * Ped. * Ped. * *Ped. Simile*

25

The Man I Love

George Gershwin

Swing

26

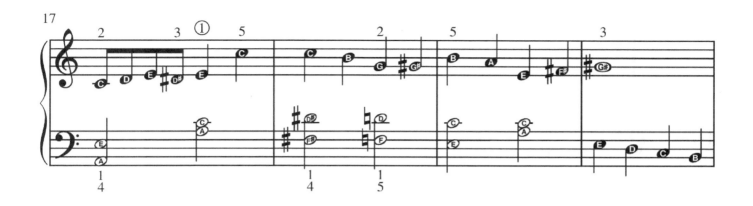

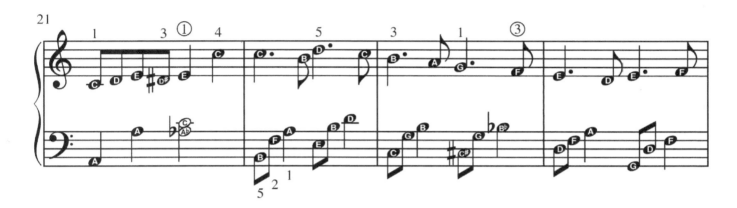

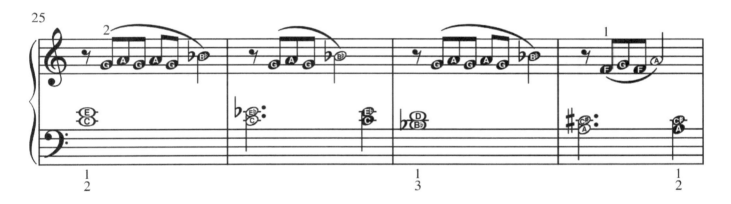

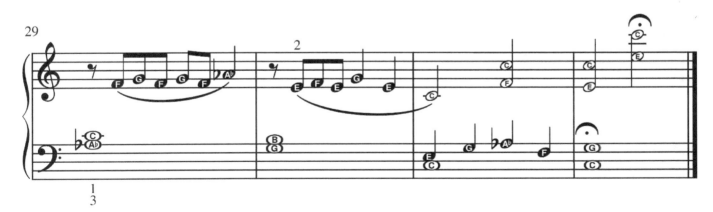

27

Embracaeble You

George Gershwin

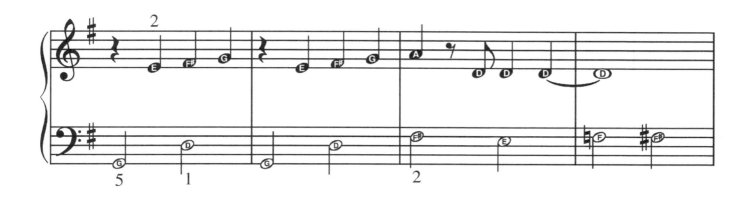

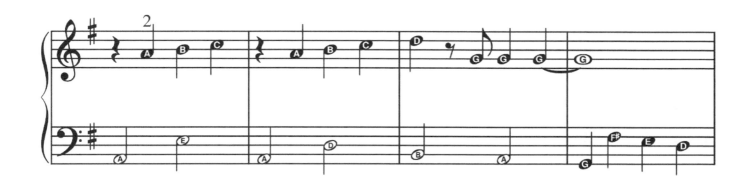

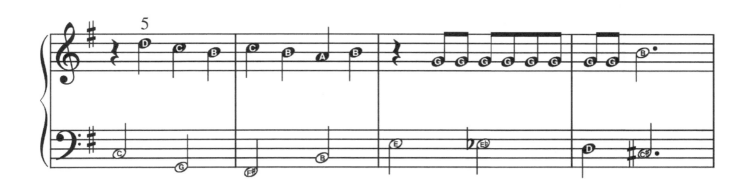

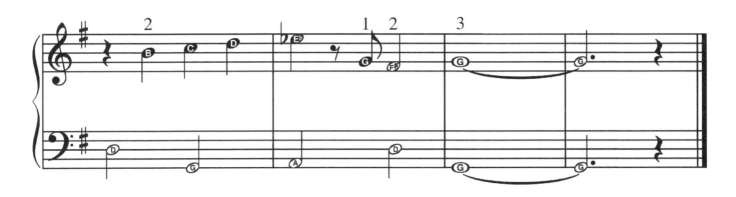

Canon in D

Johann Pachelbel

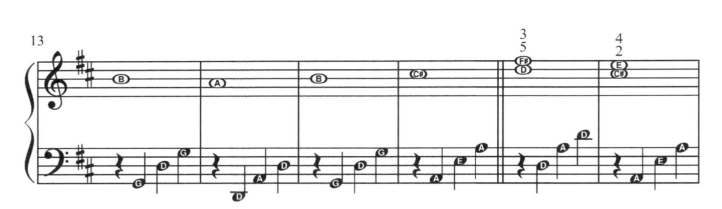

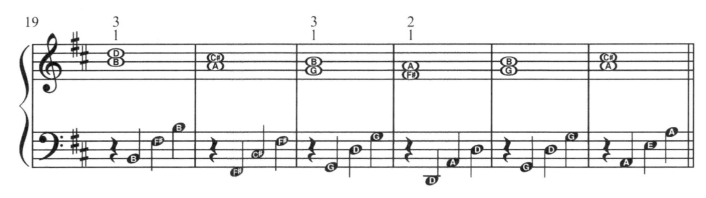

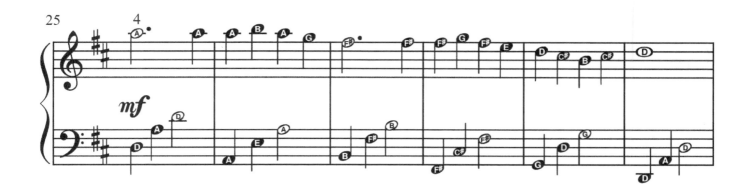

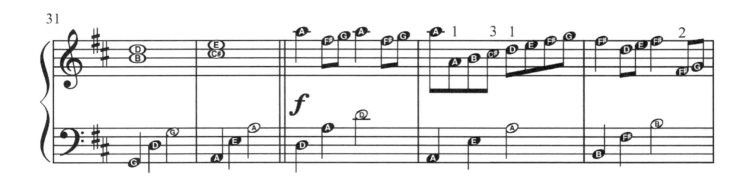

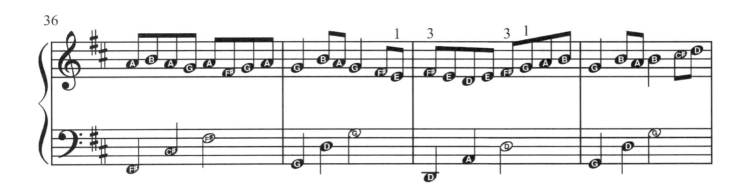

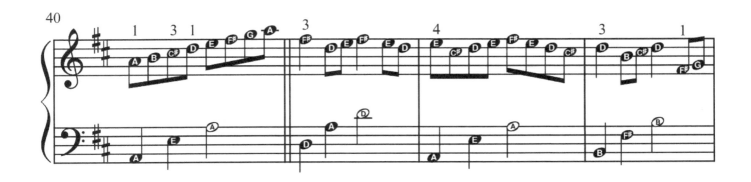

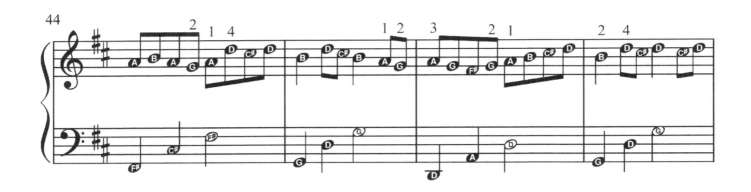

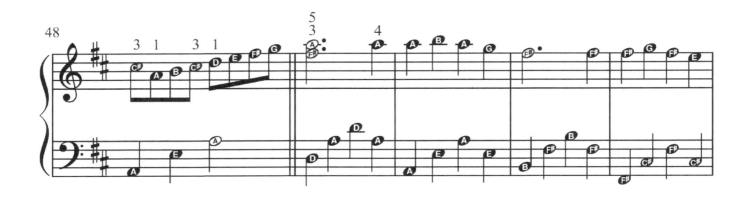

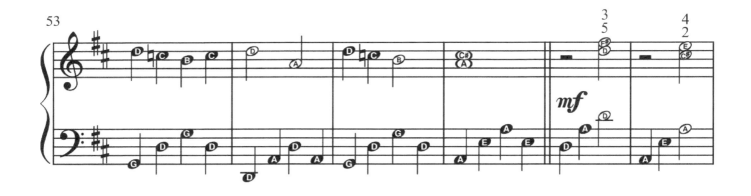

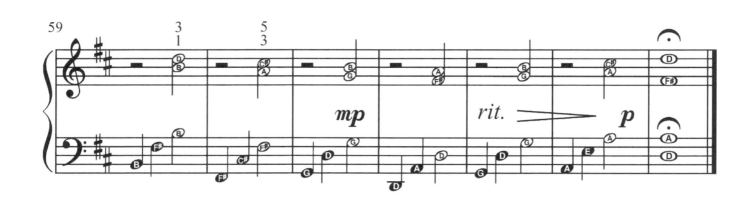

Clair de Lune

Claude Debussy

Fur Elise

Ludwig van Beethoven

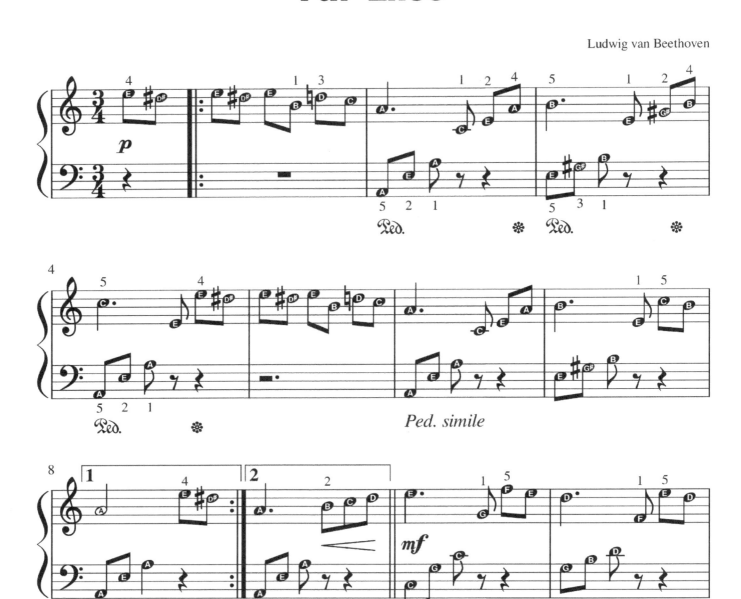

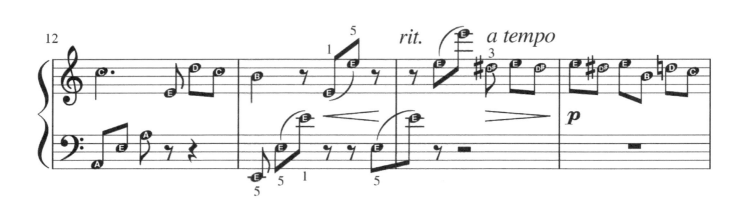

Moonlight Sonata

Ludwig van Beethoven

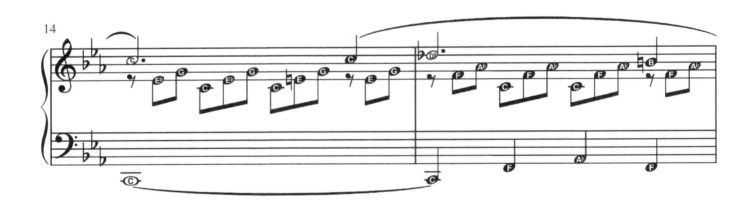

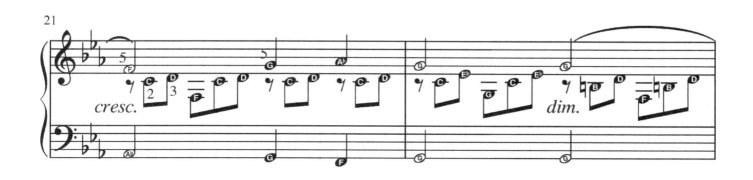

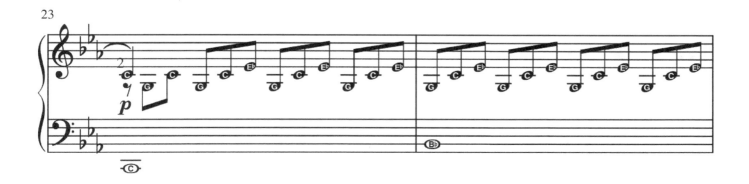

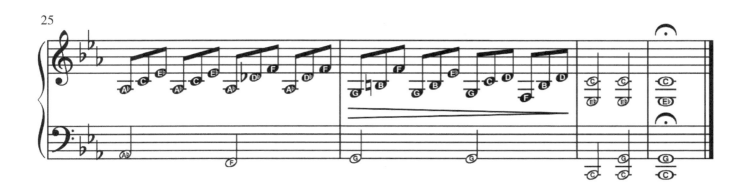

Serenade

Franz Schubert

41

O Mio Babbino Caro

from Gianni Schicchi

Giacomo Puccini

Liebestraum

from Nocturne No. 3

Franz Liszt

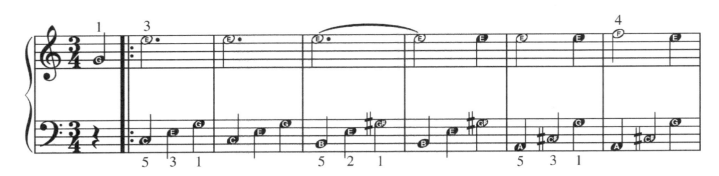

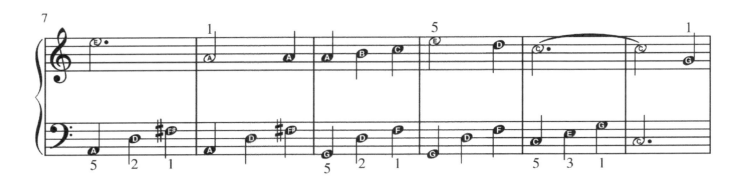

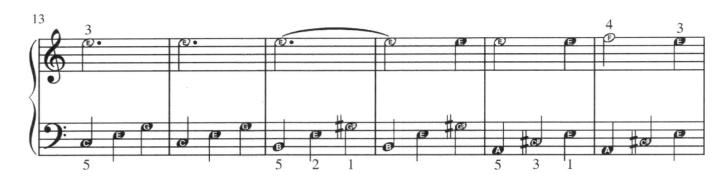

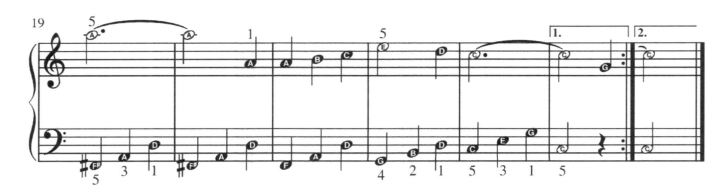

Salut d'Amour

Edward Elgar

Thank you for buying my book.
Made with passion and love.

PLEASE REVIEW
THIS BOOK

SEE OTHER ARRANGEMENTS FOR PIANO

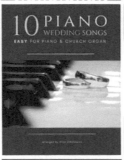

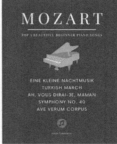
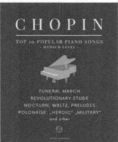
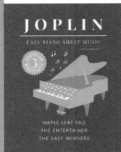

Made in United States
Troutdale, OR
12/30/2023

16543785R00031